MW00572255

iridium seeds

# iridium seeds

*poetry by*

# Sylvia Legris

For Donna
_All the best

Sylvia
April, 1999

🐦 TURNSTONE PRESS

Copyright © 1998 Sylvia Legris

Turnstone Press
607 – 100 Arthur Street
Artspace Building
Winnipeg, Manitoba
R3B 1H3  Canada
www.TurnstonePress.com

All rights reserved. No part of this book may be reproduced or transmitted in any form or by any means—graphic, electronic, or mechanical—without the prior written permission of the publisher. Any request to photocopy any part of this book shall be directed in writing to the Canadian Copyright Licensing Agency, Toronto.

Turnstone Press gratefully acknowledges the assistance of the Canada Council for the Arts, the Manitoba Arts Council and the Government of Canada through the Book Publishing Industry Development Program for our publishing activities.

Le Conseil des Arts | The Canada Council
du Canada | for the Arts
Depuis 1957 | Since 1957

Original cover artwork:
*Contemporary Meanings for Cut Flowers* (detail)
(cut flowers, pins, and text, 1995) by Joanne Bristol

Design: Manuela Dias

This book was printed and bound in Canada by Printcrafters for Turnstone Press.

Canadian Cataloguing in Publication Data

Legris, Sylvia.

Iridium seeds

Poems.
ISBN 0-88801-223-3

I. Title.

PS8573.E46175I75  1998    C811'.54    C98-920194-5
PR9199.3.L3945I75  1998

# Contents

*Resurrection music,   silence,   and surf.*

—Muriel Rukeyser

*the lung*
*blown empty*
*blossoms*

—Paul Celan
(trans. Michael Hamburger)

# I
filaments of light

discontinuous prayer

*i.  (smoke, intuition)*

after every word, a silence : to this shape, an emptiness
she can barely contain.  hold her hands in prayer, press a mark
to her heart.  this shape : silence, a prayer.
*i am the tree that trembles and trembles.*†   hear her breath.  rise.
take her hand, wipe her words off glass :

*mother, oh*

see you through the dining-room window, bending
to the light —tremulous, your lips   a tremor, your eyes
(*how many ways can you name iris?   flag-lily, liver-lily, snake-lily*),
your eyes *blue* flag,   fingers   tremble.

remember.  a broken hand (wait a day, week, month to see a doctor).
could barely hold a pen after that, handwriting fractured, crush of letters
*read this read this read my name*

*can you read my name?*

† all (in this poem) Muriel Rukeyser

\*

stick of incense.  oil on fingers, hands   pyramid your face.
smoke —intuition; sweet taste at the back of throat;
a tangle,  a

vein measures your temple : silver slide of a train.
lie in the dark, metallic taste under tongue.
ears ring.

mercury  (dis/integrate).  green-grey sky before a storm.
pressure
drop

hear your heart

*

can she hear in the dark?  single tone, the sound :
bone setting.


trace her name over granite —brush of stone.
earth settling   settle   her ribs

                              *black*

bone : density of paint (canvas thick with oil and wax),
layers
and layers

          *skin*
          *marrow*
          *ash*


drag of a pallet knife

\*

coolness : soothing. touch of skin on porcelain, forehead pressing
linoleum. turn the pillow over. (page of a book, photo album.)
this woman a restless sleeper. shift to her side back stomach.
*can't breathe*. flip the pillow. turn over over. dream
of falling.

fly. raise your arms over your head, then down. ground under you
the cool side of a pillow. leave your body in the snow.
this impression —inverse of a shadow (angel/ghost). sleep…

apnea. breath caught beneath a pillow. feathers her throat.
raise her arms over her head,

ice crystals,
air so thick    leave her body in the snow


can't see your breath

*ii.  (iridos)*

this pale light : presentiment.  hold a mirror to her lips, trembling.
this blue,   a petal to the sun,   a graft  (*endodermis, epidermis*...),   this
naked   light.

hold your hand in water.   blood; this colour, ice.  presentiment : this blue,
a breath.  this light,   an
*I.  reticulata  (flag-lily, liver-lily, snake-lily).*  this light,


\*


an iris.  press a petal to her skin —*close*
her eyes, blue : a flag.   this trace, a

light

\*

(eye   of heaven)

smell lavender on her palms.  a bloom pinned to her heart
—tincture, ghost : a mark

*past the line of memory*[†]

this pale
arc,

\*

a bridge
        between heaven &

                           earth   *(taste it can she taste it*


lie under leaves, air   pungent with sage
smell her skin, dusting of ash, shimmer of

yellow orange red   —colias wings pressed—   finger/thumb, these
traces : *iridescence*

\*

hold her breath, press   flowers on stone :  *I. reticulata.*
these marks, this   *blue below blue*† *(flag-lily, liver-lily)*.  this mark,

her eye :

the sky   rain   sea  —salt   waters her mouth                              *kiss her*
her skin,   ash  (a scar where she peels back a circle of bark),   this
mark...


hold her
heart

*iii.  (I. versicolor  —multiple heart / haiku)*

a bloom pressed beneath

her skin.  hand to her heart, her

fingers : five sepals

*

read this woman's palm.

long line of her heart, an arc

—*mother, grandmother*


*

curve   of memory.

weight of her eye a thousand

irises, a thous-

\*

-and blues   and blue,  a

crack in her eye, an escape

of air      —*word sound breath*


\*

hold her   hand, hold her.

line of her life long,   an arc.


hold her, hold her heart

*iv.   (earth, smoke)*

barely a sound; barely a word, breath.  the visible made invisible :
her heart,   a membrane of smoke, her eye,   *a-*
*gate*      —nebula :


blur of dust & gas

\*

turn in her sleep.  shape of her dream a long fall,  cascade,
its centre,  an eye  *cat aract*,       a slow

pull   of earth  —acid,  alka-
li;  metal
under skin

\*

hyaloid :                 her eye a hollow moon.

thin light through glass,   a crack
in earth,   her

heart,

\*

      agate :

stone,  breath of smoke   —this trace,
a ghost     hand  printing  earth




her touch, her

(*touch her*)

*v. (earth turn)*

*a breath after nothing*[†]


after nothing, a breath,   earth
turn beneath her,       hand
to her heart, heat rise—
is      does she hear?  ear
to earth; her      hear
her heart, her
heart,
here


hear : a breath   (her)

markers

*i.*

your hands are stone.

two elms cast shadows over you.

lines radiate your body, face,      cracks

circle your eyes

*ii.*

lie on a blanket from the sally ann.      [i am tracing your name
      over granite]

the grass is sweet, rain   sticky under heat.

what do you see?

*iii.*

what *does* she see?


filaments of light pierce the surface.

                              face streaked with sun, an

      ill ...

            you


try
to breathe
—every pore in your body blocked,
face streaked with

                              [gelatin silver print:
            hair coiled in braids —taking bread from the oven]


your face

*iv.*

stone

i am chipping away
eyes, mouth, chin


—cannot remember the curve of her jaw




*v.*

*the dates are wrong*
                              [old polaroid:
            emulsion shifting   face, hands, line of her body]


how can you tell?
how can you



*tell*
      *me*

*vi.*

stone-dust on fingers.

                                      [trace her name in dirt]

she is digging
      and
      digging,   mud

under nails

palms
damp

 

*vii.*

trace your name over granite

two elms cast shadows

hands      stone

# II

## black light  (covers her heart)

black light  (covers her heart)

*ash petals*


in a dream she watches a man spread tar
—perimeter of a graveyard
black iris growing, glowing

vision   sharpen.


names of her dead before her

eliza
anna
evelyn


*

this is a dream:

arrangement of bones


      *femur tibia fibula patella*


a corolla


her body
an eye

\*

*tighter than six feet of earth*

still there:

woman with chemicals for blood
pushing                                        walls
                                                      *of text*
                                                      *constrain her*


                    [her daughter in a bathroom throwing up
                       sometimes does this to remember]


so tired, she's unable to undo her shoes scrapes her ankles through tight laces.

she is swimming underground, arms pushing, lungs
swelling earth



pores
filters
to body



                    (*air water fire . . .*)



every cell

a truth

\*

dreaming underground:


drowning in opaque glass,
drowning again



again

*

watch the sun through rectangles of welder's glass[1]

years ago, february
—solar eclipse
standing in the centre of lake winnipeg


my mother
behind drawn curtains


                              CRY-

                                        O-



mother[2]



                              [*cryostat*][3]




[1]tissue on a slide
[2]frozen
[3][section biopsy]

\*

*nails digging into bark for dear life*

(still)

this is where it stops,
blood   seeping   mud,
cracks
the earth.

these are my mother's hands,
skin a veneer

      (i am writing a poem she is painting
       i am kneading bread she is

these are her hands          glazing cinnamon buns)

lines   arcing thumbs

      branch

           into wrists

\*

(this is) where it stops:

writing a poem about my mother

                             (she is painting
                             flowers on the wall behind the mantel:

                             scarlet flax

                             coneflowers

                             lobelia

(this is)   where
         it begins

                             blooms

                             bleeding:

*

[iridium seeds (*i-rid'-e-um*) : small particles of the metallic
element iridium, which can be implanted in the body at the
site of cancer to irradiate cancerous tissue from within]


july—
heat suffusing
my mother's skin a mesh                    (a mess)

we hang the hammock in the front porch     (body from a hook)
wrap the netting around you
a second skin                              (first skin)


        swing

            swing[4]


[4]pendulum   my mother suspended
 a pose in the mirror how i chew my lip carry my body

\*

*anna fisher: c. 1900*


anna poses in a potato field
hands wipe mud down apron

after dinner cleans her nails
pushes cuticles back
flat end of fork


                    (her brother does scales before bed
                     hand over hand black white
                     black white
                     fingers
                                    methodical



anna has perfectpitch
feels wind whistle bone
thin tone
pierce
ear

                    (*hold the knife*
                     *away from you*
                                         her mother

                     peels potatoes into a bucket
                     anna hunched listens   hears
                     sharp blade
                     train
                     passing

[air in photograph is grey]

        field cold
        anna holds     note

         train in body

        ears sharp
        feet flat   tuning

        the ground

*

*spirit lamp*


two weeks before my mother dies     [skin   white   as a]
speaks with her grandmother   *a shadow*
*anna's left lung black light covers her heart*

tells of the house she grew up in
anna in the kitchen making borscht   *mud under nails*
*season of beets staining palms*

*anna wakes in the middle of night hears piano music*
*at the top of the stairs lights a candle*   my mother
loses breath after one flight[5]


                                        *can you talk to the dead?*


[5] *her father out of nowhere fingers sheetmusic   spirit*
*-lamp   tremble air*   (wake
smell his breath
in her mouth)

*listening with the whole body*

*

*rhythms of language voicelessly passed*

listen, listen.

ear to the ground, sound
my grandmother
stirs[6]


a woman down the street gave her several packets of flower seeds
—lift her spirit


"can you remember her voice?"


(*you do what the doctors tell you*)   this is how

she taught me

to plant:


cineraria: tender perennial, cover lightly with soil  (*two fingers
      deep*)

her irises changing colour with the light  (*see how they turn their heads
      to the sun?*)


[6]simmer surface simmering
  saturdays make borscht from the backyard beets

lifts     her spirit

cineraria: tender

perennial[7]

[7]each spring we bring her
flowers   ash   petals colour skin

[cinerarium]

\*

*bones : almost discernible*


poses with her brother for a man under black  [a woman
staples blankets over windows is
listening through eyes she is   *smile*   smiling]
*smile for the . . .*

all she sees   black
light   glaring pupils


       [test a test      attest

                          colour bars
                          ed sullivan reruns
                          judy garland

        a grid

                          *somewhere somewhere some-*


                          several
                          gradations
                          of grey

       hold

           -ing      pattern


           hol-

*ding*

*dong*

*the witch is dead*

\*

click

click

click your heels together three times
make a ...


\*

       [nuclear medicine:
        radioactive substance swallowed or injected,
        distribution watched via special machine]


\*

click:

       view-

finder

\*

<u>find</u>   <u>her</u>

      *a violent woman in the violent day*[†]

pacing

hugging her-
self,
holding a

single
breath

single

breast

      [†] Muriel Rukeyser

\*

this is a dream:

her father in the front room plays piano
—ghostchords echo stairs
*shudder*   house


[shutters
 the house:
 she shrinks under light


                                        *melting* . . .



shrieks
under

*

a dream:

her father composing
arrangement of tones


[arrangement
 of bones

half-asleep dreams ivory,
the cat downstairs pads across keys


over two hundred tones in the human body
—she's heard them, listens



in her sleep

# III
bending the seasons

# h e a r t   s t r e t c h i n g   e a r t h
### (black dreams, flowers)

(I)

wake up, wake up
she is

              [dead   a thousand years
              she is


*mummy   mummy*


              hard pressed,
              she is


mum


(II)

look at her                        washing dishes in a heat wave

            *lookit—*

her face   a slow   drip,
salt crusting lip

              [my 12th birthday she gives me
              a billie holiday album    —memory pressed
              *book/flower/white gardenia . . .*

a bloom
the side of her neck, a

tūm__

                        *. . . or*

(III)

*this . . .*


october:        plant a ribbon of bulbs around the house

hands

paper


[curling at the edges




her fingers,

(IIII)

10 words:

mother

     [an old woman, she is

mother

     digging &

mother

     digging &

mother

     digging &

mother

     turning   (she is)

mother

     turning   (she is)

mother

     turn in her_____

mother

     say it   (*shhh*)

mother

     say it   (*shhh*)

mother

(*say   it*)

[say the word with pursed lips

s    t    r    e    t    c    h    e    d

earth over her

hear her

her heart

***beatingbeating***

e    a    r    t    h

(IIIII)

ray   of   gold   (*nana radiata*)

ann-a

*aaaa*   -nna

    (watch her
     watch her

           lying on the ground beside the fence

sun                     *no sense*

the sun

           makes no
           sense

(IIIIII)

stretch along the hedges,   listen
to the earth

          [hear her breathe

          under-
          ground

(IIIIII)

*listen*:

plant irises in october

                                 [*consider the moon*

barely morning
—her breath rises
white,   irises
blue ice

(IIIIIII)

consider the moon:

not an absence of light, a diffusion

                                 [*one hand shadow the other*

she is digging
      and
      digging

                            —*and this and this and*—

(IIIIIIIII)

this:

calliopsis   needs sunny exposure


anna
*ann-a*


                                [*ray   of*_____



fingers curl
at the edges

hands

paper
        /white

lungwort

1.

> *turning the twig of a   word: releasing its*
>
> *silences.*[†]

bending the seasons,   her back
winding bone  —a trellis.   her breath,

hot stretch of july
turning earth, turning

august


2.

lunge
of breath :      a gust


        the wind–

(*oh . . .*)

                open
                *gushofa*


lung,   collap
                -sing

                the air


[†] Gustaf Sobin

3.

*Pulmonaria saccharata*

sting of her breath,   sweet
smell

of  [death]


4.

wind *clapping*   —aghast, a

last gasp

                    (at last),


5.

the air, singed   —sting
of smoke.

a ghost,   her back

ben-
      ding       the wind

sinking
earth,   her
breath
turning
(turn),

strawberry geranium

strawberry geranium :    *mother of thousands*

a girl she picks dandelions, bluebells,
lily of the valley   —yard overrun

*those are weeds those are weeds you've brought*


her mother
a bouquet

thousand weeds a thousand weeds *a thousand times*
*how many times*


\*

a thousand

children, a thous-
and

this
and
this
and


\*

a thousand names (how *does*
your garden grow?):

      *echinacea*
      *witch hazel*
      *ginseng*

\*

those are weeds (this is
a dream:

strawberry geranium   will grow and multiply
grow and multiply
desert or swamp

hardy cluster side of her neck

*cut it out cut it out*

                             [prettily
                               variegated]


\*

mother of thousands

all she requires
a little shade
a mild winter

(and
this
and
this
and

    )

st john's wort

1.

> *out of those wild in-*
> *visible circuits ...*[†]

turning the earth, turning
her head

follow      a light, her eyes
pin-
      points

> *press of ink on skin*
> *thinnest nib of a pen*


2.

yellow; red;
the sky,   a taint of turpentine


clear the air :

blood / ghost
                        her hands, crimson   —tinc-
ture,
root

turn of a
word


[†] Gustaf Sobin

3.

(clear the air)

turn away from the flash.   her flesh
patches
                    of/light

eyes,   blood-
spots


            tannin &
            oil



a residue




4.

*Hypericum perforatum*   (above an ikon)

above her heart,   earth
a   r<sup>u</sup>pt<sub>u</sub><sup>r</sup>e


                    —thread


the air

\*

breathe.   her hands
red,   tinge
of balsam

             *—spirit,  gho . . .*

5.

read her palm,
wild shoots :

*life*,

        *fate*,

         *heart*

6.

leaf-
scar,
residue :


ash,

blood


(feint   of heart)

*mother of . . .*

she is cutting flowers

      *strawberry geranium*
      *strawberry geranium*

a thousand heads

fall


\*

this is a dream:

her mother reads her nursery rhymes
four and twenty blackbirds

cut . . .

*mother of*
*oh mother of*
*oh*
*mother*


\*

how does your garden
how do you
do?

*variegated*
*variegated*

                      *[prettilyprettilyprettilyprettily]*

\*

this is, uh,

a

## HAPPY ENDING   (*say it don't    say   it*) :

> *They sent for the king's doctor,*
> *Who sewed it on again,*
> *And he sewed it on so neatly,*
> *The seam was never seen.*

\*

quitecontraryquitecontrarythis ...

# IV
marginal notes  (adventitious roots)

orris  (*I.* X*germanica* var. *florentina*)

everything clings—

roothair,

earth,

words

bury her,

her eyes

deep

*consider this   the moon   an eye rising, the horizon*
*this clear line   (a lid closing and closes and   and . . .*

*an iris*
*fall*

*falls*

*& her eyes : glass      vitreous*

\*

humour her

marginal notes

*this is the world/not these words/*
*not this poem/this is the world* —bp Nichol

1.
she plants plastic k-mart flowers in the snow  *(iris, tulip)*                    *kiss*
                                                                                  *her*

from the road
red and blue a blur                                                              *kiss*
                                                                                  *her*

—trick of the seasons
a trick
of the senses                                                                    *kiss her*
                                                                                  *[death]*


\*

everything moves so fast

\*

a writer friend says these poems are too earnest

                                        (when my mother dies
my brother and i dance a do-se-do round the kitchen table · *ding dong*
*the witch is dead   swing your partner . . .*)

"where's the irreverence?" she asks

                                                                        *cut it*
                                                                        *here*

silence                                                                 *cut it*
                                                                        *there*

(dead
silence)


                                                                        *cut it*

                                                                        *in the middle*

2.

enough need-
ling.

i spend years pinning my mother

                                    (see,
there she is, in the relaxing chamber,
head a distant bob.
this is not the love boat,
this is love/is *this*____?).


in a killing jar a few drops of acetone (nail polish remover)
—a slow stun.

i paint my mother with nail polish, periwinkle blue (lungs brim with seaweed
         and brine).


norman bates norman bates, is it true a mother is a son's best friend?
what about a daughter's?

she is drumming her nails on a kitchen counter ceramic tiles a mahogany

cough
cough


even from six feet under i hear her ...


***shut up***
***shut***
***up***

3.

turn 360 degrees

add earth 1 shovelful at a time

stir   until silent

                    (dead silent)




                                        [was that




                                        irreverent?]

foxglove  (*digitalis*)

1.

      *what rushes, rushes wordless, now,*†

bloody digits, bloody bells
rings on her fingers, a hand
pulses
her heart

drain the blood from her face,
draw the shade   —night

quaking,


2.

      *earth*
      *tremor*
      *breath*


3.

dream under ground,  her

hands   shaking   (hear the earth)      *crack*

her heart,   a   wake,   a...


    † Gustaf Sobin

4.

everything said :
nothing,


a breath


(*what rushes, rushes wordless, now,*)

# Acknowledgements

Some of this writing has previously appeared in *Arc*, *The Capilano Review*, *Contemporary Verse 2*, *Grain*, *Prairie Fire*, and *Prism International*.

"black light (covers her heart)" was published as a chapbook, *ash petals*, winner of the 1996 Mother Tongue Press Poetry Chapbook Award. This same sequence was broadcast in 1996 on CBC Radio Saskatchewan on *The Arts (W)rap* and *Gallery* —my thanks to Dave Redel, producer, and his bag of technical effects.

"iridos," from "discontinuous prayer," won the 1997 Bliss Carman Poetry Award, co-sponsored by *Prairie Fire* and the Banff Centre for the Arts.

Thank you to the Saskatchewan Arts Board and to the Ontario Arts Council's Writers' Reserve Program for financial assistance that bought me time to develop this collection.

\* \* \*

I can only begin to express my gratitude to the following people who have been supportive in various ways —through their friendship, generosity of spirit and at times space, and insightful responses to this work: Susan Andrews Grace, Di Brandt, Marie Bristol, Tonja Gunvaldsen Klaassen, Amelia Itcush, Jeff Keller, Christopher Lefler, Tim Lilburn, Sandhya Padmanabh, Carla-marie Powers, Trevor Robertson, Steven Ross Smith, Sue Stewart, Maureen Varro, Jane Wagner, Betsy Warland, Rachel Zolf.

Thank you also to everyone involved with Sage Hill's 1995 Fall Poetry Colloquium, held at St. Peter's Abbey in Muenster, Saskatchewan, where much of this work fell into place.

And thanks to Stephen McLeod et al. who run the Arts Lab at the University of Saskatchewan for allowing me access to spiffy computer equipment.

Finally (but in no way least), I am grateful to Todd Bruce, who worked with me on the final editing of *iridium seeds*, for his poetic and aural virtuosity, and to Manuela Dias and Patrick Gunter at Turnstone for their diligence and support well beyond the call of duty.

self-portrait with rice krispies square